OLLIE OX
the _and_ Other Animal Tales

Illustrated by Vanessa Toye
Cover design by Phillip Colhouer
© 2021 Jenny Phillips
goodandbeautiful.com

OLLIE THE OX

Written by

Kathy Leckrone

CHALLENGE WORDS:

weighs

months

This is a musk ox. His name is Ollie. He lives in Alaska where it is very cold. He is so happy to live in the Arctic!

Ollie loves
the icy cold.

He likes the white
fluffy snow too.

Ollie has thick brown hair that almost reaches the ground! It helps him stay warm. Can you guess what is under his long coat?

Ollie has soft wool under his hair. It is eight times warmer than sheep's wool! His wool keeps him cozy and warm in the snow.

Ollie is very big. He is five feet tall. His long, dense coat makes him look even larger. Ollie is also very heavy. He weighs 660 pounds!

Do you see the short, curled horns on
each side of Ollie's head? His horns are
still growing and may end up as long as
twenty-four inches!

Ollie likes to eat grass. He likes to eat seeds. He likes to eat roots and berries too. When it is warm, it is easy for Ollie to find grass to graze on and wildflowers to eat.

But in the winter, Ollie must paw through the cold, wet snow with his large hooves to find food. It is hard work to dig in the heavy snow! Ollie uses his nose to help him search for food.

When it is winter, musk oxen stay in areas where the snow is not very deep. Do you think Ollie eats more food in the summer or in the winter?

Ollie eats most of his food each summer. This allows him to store fat, which keeps him warm in the bitter cold months when food is hard to find.

To help him stay warmer in the winter, Ollie needs to find more musk oxen. Ollie travels the frigid Arctic with his herd. A herd is a group of animals. They are like his family.

There are nine musk oxen in Ollie's herd. Six of them are Ollie and his family: his mother, his father, his sister, and his two brothers.

There is another family of musk oxen in his herd too. This is Ollie's best friend, Mina, and her parents.

Mina's mother will give birth to a baby, called a calf, very soon. A female musk ox, like Mina's mother, will have a calf after eight long months. Baby musk oxen are born in April, May, and June each year.

The young calf will walk, feed, and be ready to travel with the herd in just a couple of hours!

Together, the herd will graze on tasty grass and tiny seeds during the rest of the summer.

Once winter arrives, Ollie and his herd will travel with more musk oxen in a much larger group of sixty.

Can you guess why Ollie and his family like to travel in a bigger herd during the coldest months?

It is much easier to keep warm in the winter with the body heat of many musk oxen huddled close. This also helps them keep each other safe.

Staying warm in the arctic weather is not the only thing that Ollie must do. He and his herd must watch out for animals that hunt musk oxen. Wolves and grizzly bears are big threats!

Ollie's herd will form a circle with their sharp horns facing out and the young musk oxen safe inside.

If a wolf or bear tries to attack, Ollie and his herd will be ready!

Musk oxen like Ollie can live for up to twenty years. There are about 120,000 musk oxen in the world today.

Most of them live in the frigid Canadian Arctic. They can also be found in Norway and Russia.

Musk oxen are well suited for the icy cold climates in which they live.

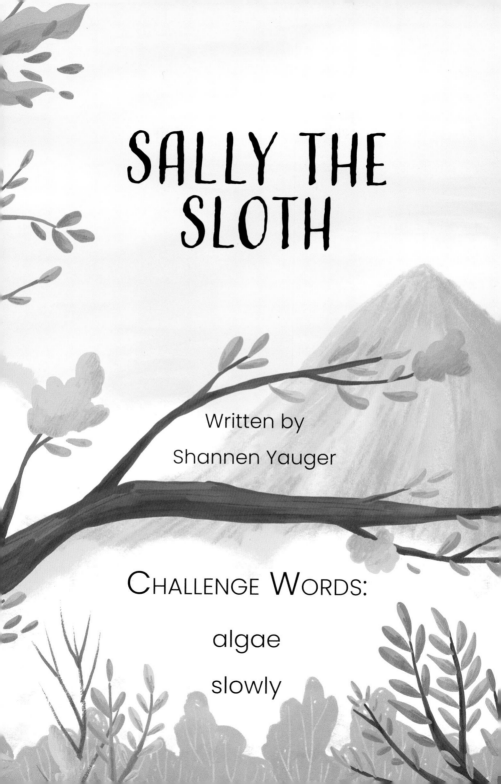

SALLY THE SLOTH

Written by

Shannen Yauger

CHALLENGE WORDS:

algae

slowly

This is Sally. Sally is a sloth. Sally spends most of her day sleeping up high in the rainforest trees. She sleeps about fifteen hours each day!

All sloths have round heads, big eyes, tiny ears, and short, stubby tails. They also have algae that grows on their backs! This helps them blend in with the trees.

Do you see Sally's claws? She has two toes on her front feet, so she is a two-toed sloth.

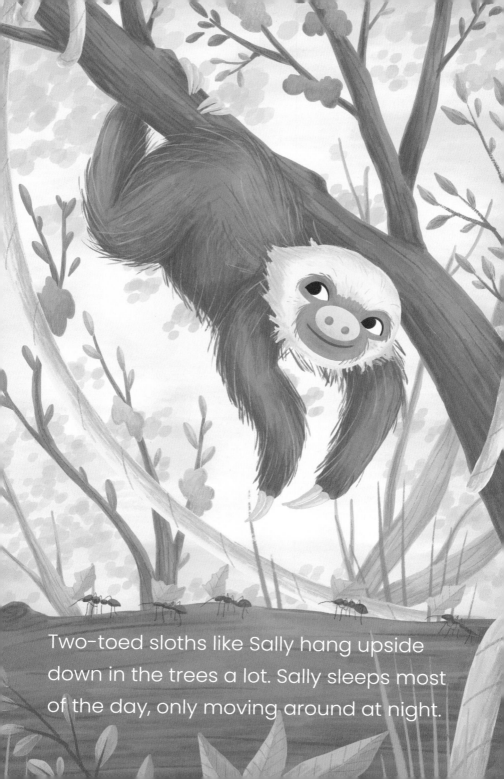

Two-toed sloths like Sally hang upside down in the trees a lot. Sally sleeps most of the day, only moving around at night.

Sally is not very big. She is only about two feet tall and weighs about seventeen pounds. Her shaggy fur makes her look bigger than she is.

Sally spends most of her life in the trees, where she is safe. She comes down from the trees only about once every other week.

When Sally is awake, she spends her time munching on tree buds, twigs, and leaves. She does not have teeth, so she chews by smacking her lips together.

Sloths do not need much to eat. The little bit that Sally does eat keeps her full for a long time.

Sally moves very slowly through the trees.
Since sloths do not eat a lot, they do
not want to use up too much energy by
moving fast.

Sally may move slowly most
of the time, but if she feels
scared, she moves fast!

She will protect herself by
slashing her claws, biting,
hissing, and screaming!

Sally also moves fast in the water. All sloths are great swimmers!

This helps them during flooding, and they swim faster than they normally move in the trees.

Do you see the sloth there in the next tree? That is Sally's mother. After Sally was born, she clung to her mother's belly. She needed to do this since she could not feed herself yet.

Sally will stay close to her mother for two to four years. She still has a lot to learn from her mother.

Sally does not see very well. All sloths cannot see color, and they only see a little bit in dim light. When the sun is bright, they are blind!

Sally, like other sloths, does have a great sense of smell and a really good memory! This helps make up for not being able to see and allows her to move around safely.

Across the rainforest, we find Steve. Steve is also a sloth, but do you see his claws on his arms? He has three front claws, so he is called a three-toed sloth.

Steve is a little bit smaller than Sally and is only twenty-three inches tall. He also is not as shaggy as Sally. Where Sally is often upside down, Steve likes to sit up in the fork of the tree.

Unlike Sally, who moves slowly through the rainforest at night, Steve still lives in the same tree where he was born.

He moves very slowly from branch to branch in his tree during the day, turning his head almost all the way around to see and smell what is near him.

Both Steve and Sally are amazing sloths. These slow-moving animals are so much fun to watch if you can spot one hidden in the trees of their rainforest home.

ADAM THE ANTEATER

Written by

Shannen Yauger

CHALLENGE WORDS:

swallows
termite
tongue
minute
jaguar
wrists

Look over there, through the grassland.
Do you see that big animal? It is Adam
the anteater!

Adam is a giant anteater. He is almost eight feet long!

Giant anteaters do not eat just ants!
Adam likes to munch on termites too.

Giant anteaters like Adam have long snouts that help them to get to their food. Inside Adam's snout is a long tongue. His tongue starts inside his body and can extend to two feet long!

Adam's long tongue is very sticky and has spines on it. To eat, Adam puts his snout to the ground and sucks the ants onto his tongue.

He then swallows the ants whole since he does not have teeth.

Adam can eat up to thirty thousand ants and termites each day!

He will feast at a nest for only about a minute before moving on to the next nest.

He does this so he does not have time to be bitten or stung by the insects in the nest. Adam will visit up to two hundred nests in a day!

Adam has long claws. He uses these claws to open up ant and termite nests.

Adam's claws are so long that he needs to walk on his wrists so he does not poke himself.

Adam strolls through the grassland, shuffling along with his nose to the ground.

Giant anteaters cannot see very well, so Adam uses his sense of smell to find his way to his next meal.

Adam is full, so he curls up to rest. It is cool in the grassland today, so he digs a shallow hole in the ground, curls up, and folds his bushy tail over his body. This will help him stay warm.

Look across the grassland! There you will see Anna the giant anteater. She stays far away from Adam, as she has a baby on her back.

While anteaters do not like to be around other anteaters, Anna will carry her baby on her back for nine or ten months. By then the baby will be able to care for himself.

Do you see how the baby blends into Anna's fur? This makes the baby easy to hide, and that will help keep him safe.

It is dark now, and Adam is walking to the water hole. He will sit in the water hole for a bath, which will help him get rid of any ants or termites stuck in his fur.

While he does not do it often, Adam is also a strong swimmer. He uses his snout as a snorkel and can swim for miles in the river.

Morning has come again, and Adam starts to look for food. Wait! What is that animal lurking in the tall grass?

Do you see the jaguar that is sneaking up on Adam? Adam cannot move away, so he stands up on his hind legs and bares his claws.

Adam looks big and scary! The jaguar stops and watches Adam.

Adam leans against his tail and swipes at the air with his claws!

The jaguar runs off. Adam drops back down on all four legs and gallops away. He will find a new area to hunt in today.

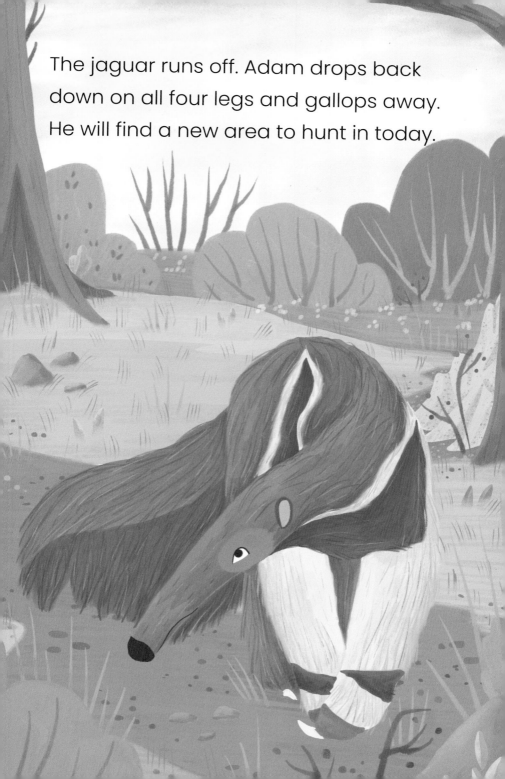

Check out these other Level 2 books from The Good and the Beautiful!

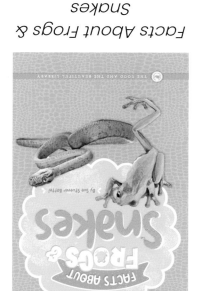

Facts About Frogs & Snakes
by Sue Stuever Battel

Brave Little Ruby
by Shannen Yauger